A Daughter's Book of Secrets

A Daughter's Book of Secrets

*Things a Dad Should Tell His Daughter
before She Leaves Home*

Robin K. Johnson

RESOURCE *Publications* • Eugene, Oregon

A DAUGHTER'S BOOK OF SECRETS
Things a Dad Should Tell His Daughter before She Leaves Home

Resource Publications
An Imprint of Wipf and Stock Publishers
199 W. 8th Ave., Suite 3
Eugene, OR 97401

www.wipfandstock.com

PAPERBACK ISBN: 978-1-4982-9215-3
HARDCOVER ISBN: 978-1-4982-9217-7
EBOOK ISBN: 978-1-4982-9216-0

Manufactured in the U.S.A.   JULY 21, 2016

To all my daughters: Chrishanda, Leah, Jesika-Dyann, Judietta, Jenifer, Amber Rae, Cailyn, Mikkel, Rebekah, Melissa, and Jaleesa

To the staff and volunteers of Bay Area Turning Point Webster, Texas

—YOU LADIES INSPIRE ME

Contents

Foreword

Is there a life experience more beautifully traumatic than a father watching his children grow up?

The transition typically happens over a long period. A newborn daughter may enjoy the tight swaddle of her father, but then over the years, celebrated milestones will begin a process of separation: first steps, first words (and thus first spoken opinions like "Mine!") The child goes to kindergarten. A friend invites her for a sleepover. Eventually, she is riding her own bike to soccer practice, or playing the flute on stage by herself and dad is limited to the role of spectator. Puberty transforms the relationship with dad in both exciting and uncomfortable ways. At some time, love and dating enter the picture, bringing fathers to entire new levels of protective instincts.

And then suddenly, in cruel brevity, a father's eighteen-year dance of nurturing independence culminates in this young girl becoming a woman and the mundane parts of that independence often bring lots of anxiety to poor dad. Many dads have held back tears while helping their daughter move into a new dorm, new apartment, new life.

Robin's words represent all that fathers want to give to their daughters. He covers the practical advice from car maintenance to apartment safety precautions. He even ventures to areas of hygiene and "dropping kids off at the pool," a conversation most often avoided by teenage daughters. But after this pragmatic advice, Robin focuses on a set of spiritual principals, based on biblical texts. He encourages his daughters to consider the wisdom of Scriptures and to let these texts guide and protect in ways that he can no longer do.

I remember Robin in my biblical studies classes, as he learned historical critical approaches to biblical texts and as he worked on exegetical assignments. He was interested in biblical interpretation and contexts, but I most remember how so much of his learning was tied to his own self-identity as a father.

I believe that this book is a reflex of Robin's own experience as a theology student and father. As I read his words, I imagine him in his home, surrounded by pictures of his children, recalling both pride and regret as a father. I imagine that Robin's writing of this book was therapeutic in that by giving these words to his daughters, he is still with them, wherever they go in this world. Yes, perhaps he wrote this for himself and for dads around the world.

It is a message written through a labor of love to be shared with others.

Dr. Roger S. Nam, Ph.D.
Associate Professor of Biblical Studies
George Fox Evangelical Seminary

Foreword

On the desktop of my computer lies a file called "The Wisdom of Dad." This file holds a collection of cartoons, pithy sayings, and sage advice from my father. It is evidence of his deep love for me, usually in comic form. I click on the file every now and then and as I read I can hear his voice, a voice that has saved me from disaster so many times. It is a voice that I ignore at my own peril. In my office there is another bit of evidence of my father, a file labeled "Communications." This file holds bits and pieces of hand written love sent through the mail over the span of my lifetime, and they are precious to me. When I need to be reminded of who I am, my father's words pull me back to center. How often I have wished for a compilation of these words, along with the many that were spoken yet never written.

A father has the power to hold a daughter in a way that no one else can, not even a mother or a good husband. The words of a father are creative. His words have the potential to spark life or cause death in the soul of his daughter and therefore must be lovingly thought out and carefully expressed. One way or the other, they will remain with her forever.

Robin K. Johnson brings his love, compassion, and wisdom to life for his daughters in A DAUGHTERS BOOK OF SECRETS. Written as a love letter, he offers a peak into the intimate discussions a father and daughter. Johnson delivers common sense priorities for everyday life expressed with humor and pragmatism, addressing everything from intimacy (you are not an amusement park ride), home safety (never take the trash out at night), relationship Oh-Oh's (he wants to borrow money?), to party safety (get your own drink to avoid roofies) and much more.

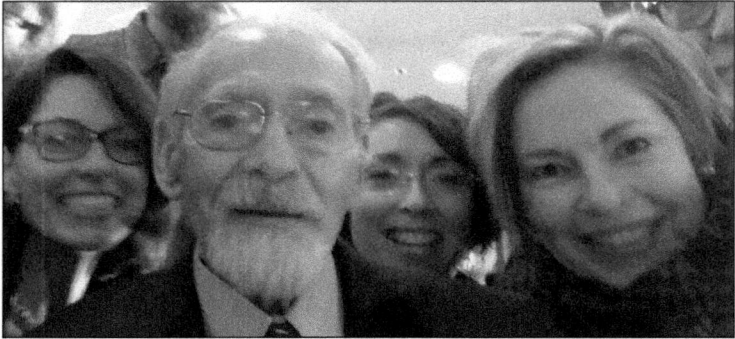

Bruce and his baby girls—Deborah, Lisa and Krissann

Johnson adds a *Consider This On This Day* section, which includes devotional readings and thoughts to nurture the souls and spirits of his daughters as they become young women of faith and citizens of the world. It becomes evident that Johnson cares more for his daughter's hearts than he does about their right or wrong doing. Speaking with grace and compassion, he says, "There is not a man on earth worth the salt in your tears." What woman on earth doesn't want that dad?

Each devotional opens a door for discussion on deep levels of identity, relationship, belonging and love, leaving ample opportunity to add your own bits of wisdom and advice to Johnson's. Although I have been an adult woman and a Christian for many years, I felt the father heart of God in a new way through Johnson's writing.

It is my hope that you will read this humorous, heartwarming, and practical book from cover to cover with your daughters. Maybe you will feel God the Father in a new way too.

Deborah Koehn Loyd, M.Div.

You Are My Flower

Here it is in a nutshell:

I love you so much that I would love to be the cheerleader in the corner when you are feeling like you do not have the strength to make it to the next minute; let alone the next day. All of my prayers, silly songs, those silly things I have done just to make you smile and what I thought was a motivational speech are in this book.

Eric & Regina

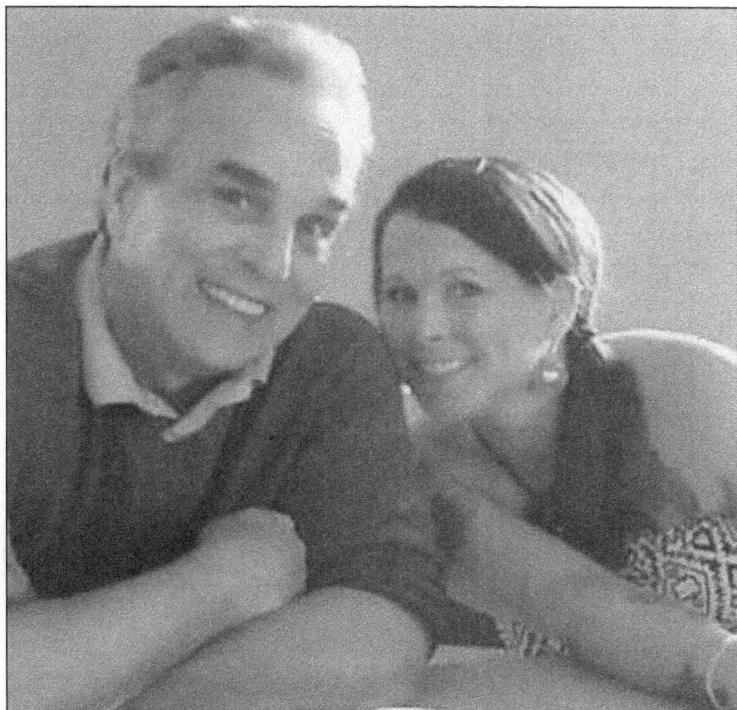

William and Mandi

Starting with this page—I want you to realize that you are AL-WAYS a force to be reckoned with and not some guy's conquest. Believe in yourself and your talents first, because in my eyes, there is not one other woman better than you. I believe in you and want the best to fall in your path.

I want you to look through it because it has some of my thoughts and dreams for you. But most of all, I want you to be well-prepared in figuring out who you would like to be after you have aligned all of your dreams and goals into one bucket. The biggest step in each of your days will begin in how you trust in yourself, God and the love I have had for you from the first day I held you, the first day you returned a hug and smile to me and through the times when we fussed and patched things back together.

It is not that I do not trust you to make it in this world. It is what this world may do to you that I do not trust.

This is not easy to see you become a queen after tending to you as MY princess all of these years. I know there has been days that I failed to make you smile, failed to say the best words to you, failed to get you the things you truly wanted and I apologize for not being able to provide you with the greatest life. But I am happy that you are my daughter. And that we had a good life together.

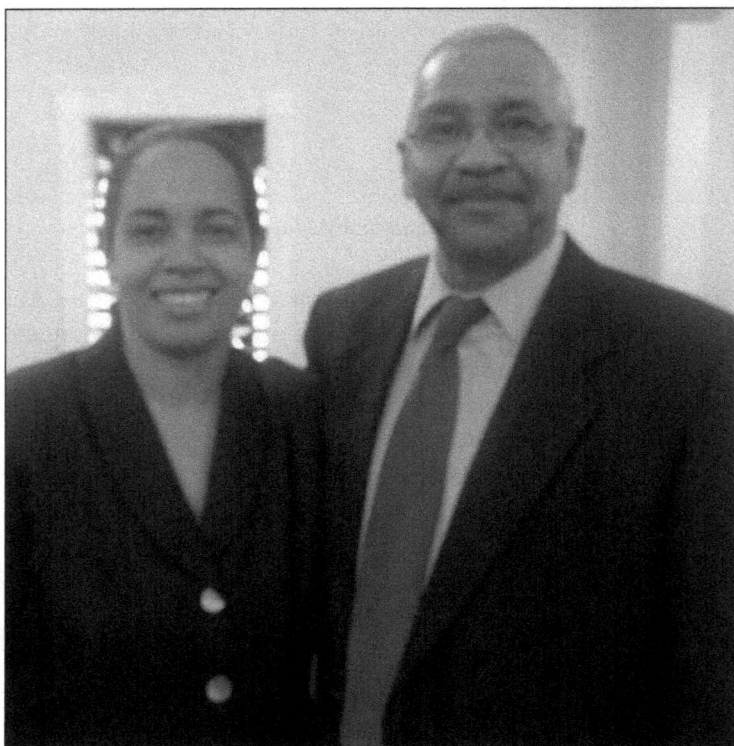

Victor and Tere'

Who You Are Is Who You Choose to Believe You Are

There will be those days where you will feel like your life is not worth living. Though it may be through circumstances out of your control or situations in which you may have or may have not made the greatest of decisions. Nothing can or should deter you from seeing how great you are in this world, how beautiful and strong you are to yourself and then to me. Life is hard and I wish I could be your daily cheerleader and assist you through the rough parts.

The pages following contain idioms in which I hope you will take a moment and write one down each week to encourage yourself when no one else is around to offer the cheers that you need to get your focus and steps back in order.

Mark, Eleanor and Grace

Nick and Halle

Chad and Riley

Denis, Ambrosia, Astin, Antonique and Amerie

I am like a Chameleon

Because I can adapt to the strangest of situations and still look better and get the job done without a pat on the back. No one needs to see me, but they know that I am the one who gets the job done.

I am like a Turtle

Because I withdraw in a moment, regroup and regain myself and still be miles ahead those in the conversation.

I am like an Eagle

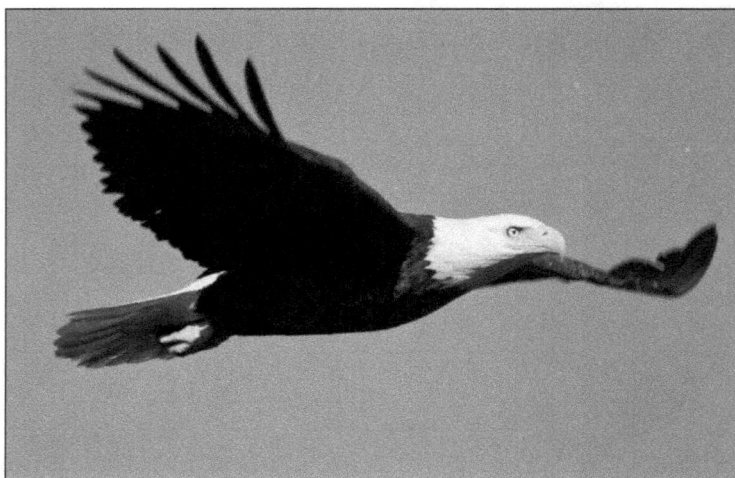

Because I can rise above the storms of life and still focus on my quests for the day.

I can soar above the little things and still take care of the majors without missing a beat.

I am like an Iceberg

Because not one person can ever understand the depths of my beauty, the strength of my character, and the power that is in all of my talents and God-given gifts.

I am like a Traffic Light

The signals that I send off are of my own choosing.

I cannot be easily swayed into changing the flow of life based on the noisy traffic coming from friends and family.

I am like the Sunrise

Because the joy and happiness I possess does not need to be qualified, quantified or checked off by anyone. I am the reason people leave my presence smiling. I am the ray of sunshine I was created to become.

I am like the Early Morning Rooster

Because I rise knowing that I have things to say during the day which will wake up, inspire and create positive thoughts in all those I love and care about.

I am the Story in an Unending Book

Because the more a person learns of me, they quickly realize that I am a page turner and the more they read me, the better they realize that I am worth better than each sentence spoken of me.

For my Best Friend
Callie and her sister Cassandra
in memory of Isaac "Big Ike" Lawson

The Boyfriend / Partner Affect

In this note, I am not trying dictate who and where you should date. I am just giving you little tidbits of information and maybe some warnings to keep you and your heart safe from being trampled on by those who victimize you for your money and sex.

Tyler and his beautiful daughter Tasha

Jamie and Jmya

The 90 Day Rule-Value

There should be a definite time that you allow yourself to get to know the person you may give your goods to. I am thinking that 90 days just be a minimum. Don't cringe; I think you have gone more than 17 years, hopefully 20 before you began engaging in physical activities of this nature. I do value you and think that you should require a higher standard than the average, "we have been dating for two weeks and no sex" conversation. You are worth more than just an experience.

You are not an amusement park ride.

It should be a matter of trust and security. The person may just be a sexual predator and have 3 or 6 children in the wings that he is not taking care of.

Anyway, the 90 days will allow you to pick up on certain habits this person has that are either unhealthy or unsafe. There are far too many diseases and baby momma's out there which cannot be unscrewed or removed by the means of obtaining a pill or a shot.

The 125 Day Rule—Possession

Here is the scenario. You are dating and the person (guy or girl) wants to borrow money during the first 30 days of you knowing them; is kind of out of sorts, right?

The key to getting beyond this and learning of them is to think on how much they want from you, when they say they will return the money to you and how many times before you have had to pay for things on the outings you have had with them.

Don't be used.

The rule of loaning money goes this way—if you cannot afford to give it away, do not loan it out. NO is not a dirty word when it comes to your finances.

This person is supposed to ready and willing to be with you for the long haul, but if it seems that you are carrying the brunt of the load for the first 6 months of the relationship, something is seriously wrong. The decision must be made to cut loose and ties with this succubus.

Here is list of Uh-Oh's and suggestions that this person is not working with a full focus on life:

- In the first 10 days, they want to know everything about your past relationships—this is a set up for how they can work you and get over
- In the first 10–15 days, they know where you keep all the things in your apartment—they plan on moving in on you in small incremental days

- In the first 15 days, the question is dropped, "can you front me $30.00 for gas?"
- In the first 20–30 days, the question comes up, "can I borrow your car?"
- In the first 30 days, you have had to pick up the bill for the dinner date on more than two occasions
- In the first 45 days, the conversation has already gotten into talk about living together
- In the first 60 days, this person moves from two jobs
- In the first 60 days, your laundry basket has more of their clothes than yours
- In the first 90 days, there have been missed dates, unreturned phone calls and messages

Robin and Amber Rae

Mark, Eleanor and Grace

Apartment and Home Safety

Your safety is paramount. This is why I am given you these point-
ers on what you should do to protect yourself.

Your Purse, Wallet, and Walk-through

This is just an *IF*; you are staying home for a while. Place your belonging in your bedroom and away from guests and visitors. Sticky
fingers are attached to all kinds of people.

When you arrive home, don't just throw your purse on the
first flat surface you see. Take a walk to your bedroom and take
notice of your things and question yourself if all things are in the
exact place where you have left them. Making this your habit will
allow you the advantage of quickly scanning rooms just in case
there is an uninvited guest in your house.

Windows

In your apartment or your house, you need to make a tour of your
windows once a week to see if they are STILL locked. I am not
saying that you cannot trust your friends, but you cannot trust
everyone you let into your personal space.

The best way to make sure the lock never fails—a flat paint
stirrer or butter knife can be slide into the gap between the windows. This will thwart anyone from entering your window through
an unlocked window. Once you make your rounds of your windows, you can quickly see if your device is still in its place and the
locks are still closed. If not, you quickly realize that you need to
change your circle of friends.

To make sure you see the stick during an emergency:

- Paint the ends of the stick / butter knife with fluorescent paint
- Tie a string with a bright colored plastic washer on the end
  and allow it to hang little ways away from the stick / butter
  knife

- Fire Drill—practice several times a year

Kitchen
A clean kitchen is a safe kitchen

Now that you have moved into your own home, please take your trash out during the day and NEVER at night.

Keep your floor swept and clear of those small piles of dirt and dust, those can be slipping hazards. I do not want to get a call from the hospital saying that you crack you head open from a fall in the kitchen

Place all your knives in the back of your kitchen drawer. I am sure that either you or I have purchased a utensil saver with the large space in the rear of the spoons and forks—this will not allow anyone quick access to your sharps without your knowledge. And if anyone wants to harm you, you will hear the draw open and thing shuffle around because they have to reach

Chairs

After you have been on your own for a while, you should check your chairs to ensure that they are still stable and clean. Look at the back corners of each chair. Remove all the dust, food any dirt which has accumulated.

You want your house to reflect how you would like others to think of you after they have left your company. Be a cleaner person than you were as a teenager (lol !)

Car Maintenance and Upkeep

A Simple Car Safety Message that will keep you safe and save you a little money. I know I hawk you about learning new things and you roll your eyes, but I know you are listening to me. So I have given you a few notes in taking care of your vehicle and yourself.

Bryan and Judietta

John, Taylor and Gabby

The Flat Tire

- Pull off the road so that you are safely out of the flow of traffic
- Try to stop in a straight part of the road, so that passing traffic can see you from a distance

NOTE: if traffic is too busy . . . drive slowly and get off at the next exit and pull over on the feeder road. We can replace a tire rim and tire.

- Stop the car on a level spot, it is unsafe to jack up a car on an incline
- Turn on your Hazard lights
- Raise your hood and trunk—this will show other motorist that you are in distress and make them aware of you on side of the road
- Retrieve the tools listed above from the car and place them within reach
- If desired, put on the gloves, and place the blocks under the tire opposite the flat
- Position the jack under the car, and raise the jack until it contacts the frame
- Make sure the jack is properly positioned
- Extend the jack until the tire is about 6 inches off the ground
- Remove the lug nuts from the bolts, and put them aside
- Grab the wheel
  - it is easiest to grab the tire at the "nine o'clock" and "three o'clock" positions
- Pull the wheel straight toward you, and off the car
- Position the spare tire directly in front of the wheel well
- Align the holes in the center of the spare tire with the bolts on the car
- Lift the spare tire and position it on the threaded bolts

- Push the tire onto the car until it cannot go any farther
- Replace the lug nuts on the bolts and tighten them, but not too tight . . . just enough to hold the tire in place while you lower the car
- Lower the car with the jack until the car is again resting on all four tires
- Tighten the lug nuts, starting with one; then moving to the one opposite it, and so on . . .
- Place the flat tire where the spare was located
- Replace the jack and lug wrench in their proper locations
- Carefully inspect your work area and make sure that you're not leaving anything
- Continue on to your destination, and have the flat tire repaired

Tires

It is important that you rotate you rotate the tires on your car once every three to four months. This will allow your tires to wear in an even patter and save on your having to purchase one tire at varying times.

This is something that will take you 25 minutes to do on your own or less than $20.00 if you go to a tire shop and have it done. OR you could give me a call and I can do it for you and we can have lunch together after I am done doing this and washing your car.

- The first time you rotate the tires—do it in an X pattern.
- The next time you rotate the tires—do it front to rear and rear to front
- The following time you rotate your tires—do it in the X pattern again
- The next time you rotate the tires—it is time to take a penny and check the tread wear

- If Abe's head in not buried in the tread, it is time to replace those tires which have been worn down

Changing Oil

This is something which should be done on a regular basis. Well, that is if you want your car to last through the last of your payments. Take your car to have the oil changed based on the manufacturer's system: every 3 months or 3,000 miles or 5 months or 5,000 miles.

Spending the $36.00 to get to get this done will save you thousands of dollars in the long run if you do not do it. It only takes 30 minutes out of one day every 3 or 5 months.

So, DO NOT SKIP ON THIS!

Turn Your Head

No matter how much I harp on certain things, which may seem like a lot at times, I just want you to live a long and happy life.

Let's talk about driving for a few minutes.

When you pull up to a stop sign or traffic light, it is really not the time to check your cellphone or concentrate on changing the music on the radio. What is most important is that you check you distance from the car in front of you.

Turn your head—is simply asking you to look around you. Take notice to where you are, who is walking on the sidewalk or even in the next vehicle. Always take a moment to ensure you have a notion of what is taking place in the immediate area.

William, III and Trene'

If you can see underneath the vehicle in front of you, then you have enough room to pull out if that car's engine stalls, someone approaches you and you need to pull out or if you are feeling ill and need to turn into the other lane to leave the area.

On the need for having
sensible shoes in your car

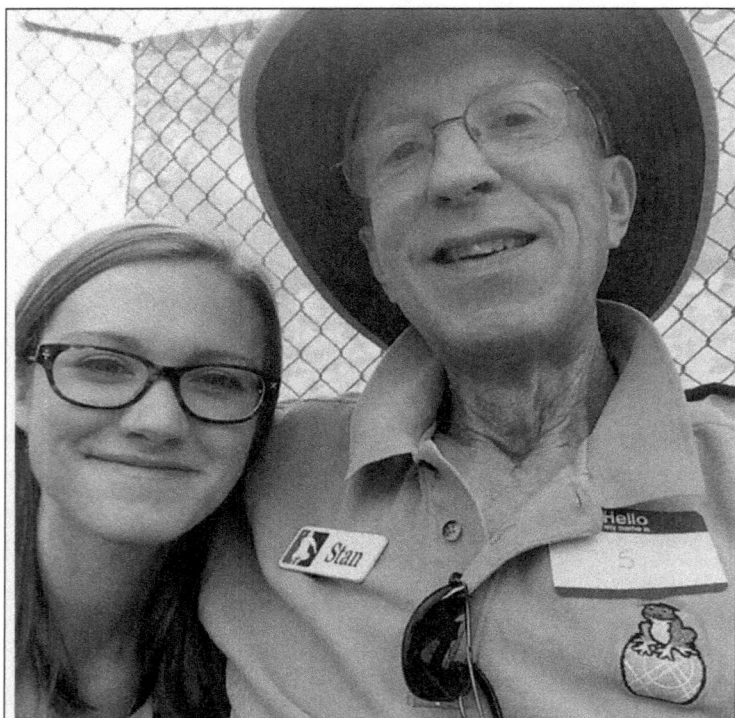

Stan and Sarah

I do know that you will create the habit of leaving shoes in the car. That is fine with me, as long as one pair is a pair of tennis shoes / sneakers. I say tennis shoes because they are better for you to walk in if you are stranded than the heels you like to wear. Keep those in the back seat or in the trunk for easy access.

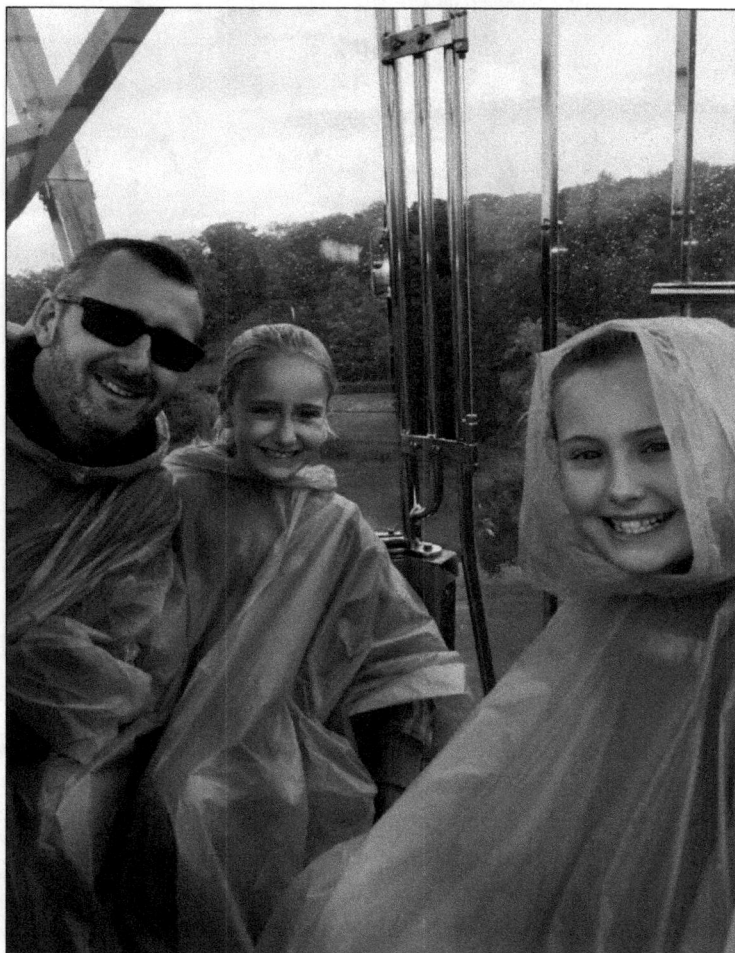

Mark, Grace and Eleanor

Upon leaving the mall, store, or theatre

Robin and Jaleesa

Whenever you are exiting a building, store or movie theatre please take note to who all is around you.

Turn your head! Get your keys and your Safety Cat out. Take notice of all things around your car—people and random objects which might cause you to take pause before getting into your vehicle. Texting can wait until you get home. Or if you have on a headset, call someone to let them know that you are about to be on your way home. I am not trying to keep tabs on you, but to allow you the comfort that someone has you on their mind and will call and check on you if you do not make it home in a timely manner.

REASON: I don't want you to take any moment for granted. Understand that there are some bad actors in this world who are bent on interrupting somebody's day with the need to hurt and take something that it not theirs to take.

Mike and Kirvin

Dadisms

I know there are some days that I talk to you and it seems like a never ending river of advice. It is not because I am trying to control you or make you a clone of me. I just simply want the best for you on every day that you are alive.

Besides that, I really want all of the things I tell you to be conversation starters. I want to be a part of your world, even if it is last the length of a 15-minute conversation.

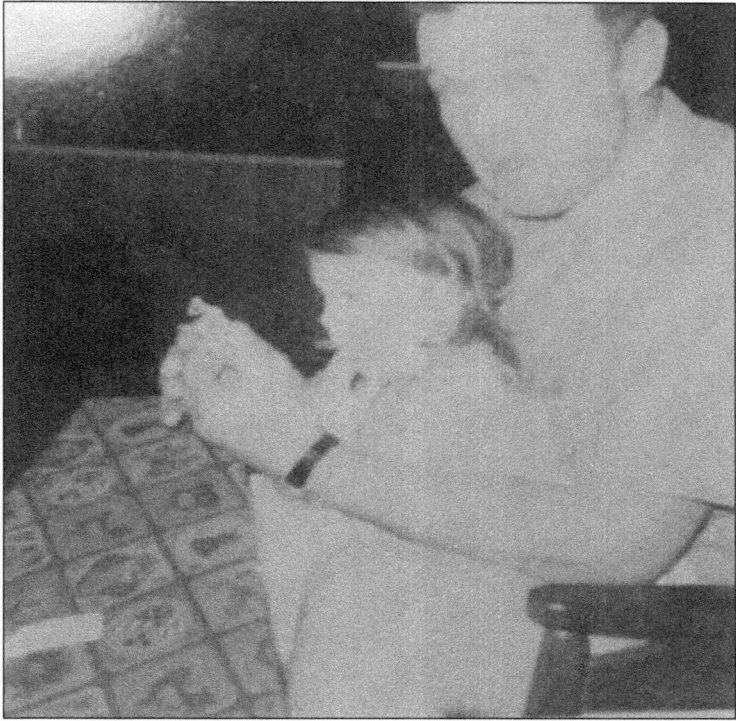

For Elizabeth in memory of Fred Felkner

On the subject of Driving

When you arrive at a stop light and you are not the first car in line, stop far enough back that you can see under the rear axle of the car in front of you. By you leaving this amount of room, if the car in front of you stalls you will have enough room to go around that car and remove yourself from being delayed in getting to your destination.

Richard and his princess Tatyana

On the issues of having an irritable stomach
which causes you to have gas . . .

Robin and Cailyn

If you are in a crowd of people or in a public space and you need to release some gas, belch instead. People will forgive you belching over smelling the mess brewing in your stomach. Belching will cause the pressure wanting to leave the lower parts of your body to move away from the escape hatch.

Reason: This will allow you the time to leave the room and get to the bathroom.

Bryan and Judietta

On the issue of you arriving home
and putting your purse down

Robin and Melissa

The location of your purse falls to the issues of trust with your friends and then some family members. And trust has to remain on the table. When you are the end of your day and you arrive home, take your purse to your bedroom and then relax and unwind. By placing your purse in your room adds a level of security for your identification and the money you have in your wallet.

Reason: not too many people will travel to your room and take something out of your purse without you taking notice.

Mat, Abigail and Elizabeth

On the issue of being a true friend

Mark, Eleanor and Grace

Most people do not understand your frustrations and struggles to remain focus and your need to be validated. They don't understand BECAUSE they won't stop talking long enough to hear your hurts and anger in the situation because they tend to interject their own stories into everyone else's world.

On the day the tables turn and you are not the subject of healing . . . Take a breath. When you are in the conversation with one of your friends and they are extremely distressed, take a breath and realize that as a friend you are required to be there to LISTEN. Please don't give your life as an example. This is not the time to do that. Allow them to breathe, cry and come to grips with the challenges they are working to understand.

REASON: I want you to understand how the heart works. The pain in the heart does not need added distractions. Emotional decisions are not well planned actions and your interjecting into someone else's challenges will not end well and solidify the friendship with the person you are dealing with.

On the issues of using public toilets

When you are out doing your favorite thing—shopping—you need to carry a small pack of baby wipes . . .

Robin and Chrishanda

I know that there will be those times that you will need to use the public bathroom. I have been in those bathrooms. You will need to take two baby wipes and clean off that seat before you put you behind down on any of them. And then that toilet paper may just be too hard and give you a papercut where you do not wish to have one. Use the baby wipe to clean up before you leave out.

REASON: Those toilets can be nasty as heck.

On the issues of taking a drink while at a party

Deepak and Avani

I really don't care if you are at a party with people you "kind of know" or work with, get up and get your own drink. Yeah, the party is on point, on fleek and you are seriously enjoying the conversation . . . get up and get your own drink.

REASON: Too many people have been slipped "Roofies" into their drinks and have been taken advantage of. Like I always say, your safety is more important to me than anything in this world.

On the issues of your teeth
and breath during the day

Nick and Halle

As good looking as you are, a moment of bad breath will kill off conversations and blow some deals in the middle of the day. Keep a travel size toothbrush and toothpaste with you to clean your mouth after you've eaten lunch.

REASON: Fresh breath and a clean smile makes a good first impression, second impression and they last for a long while after the conversation is over.

On the issue of your bathroom(s)

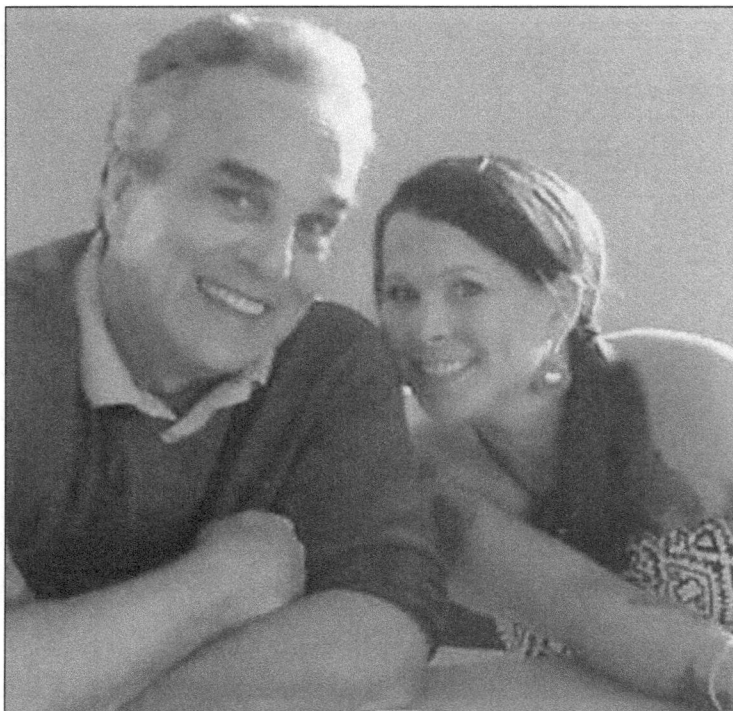

William and Mandy

The place in your house that will give people pause is the bathroom. No matter how clean that room is, if there is any type of smell being emitted from there, people will give you the "side eye" when they exit. If you are having a gathering or just a few friends over, either drop a Clorox tablet or pour a cup of bleach into the tank 30-minutes or an hour before people arrive. The fruity smelling things placed around the bathroom cannot handle the bad smell of poop directly.

REASON: if one of your guests has the bubble guts or decides to "drop the kids off at the pool" their odor will be stifled before they exit the bathroom.

On the issues of loaning money

Denis and his daughters- Ambrosia, Astin, Antonique and Amerie

When anyone has the nerve of calling you and asking for money (any amount) if you cannot afford to give it to them—then don't do it. If they are calling because their electric is about to be disconnected, loaning the money will not fix their issue of paying bills. You will become a "bill" that most likely will not be repaid. Besides all of this, those people who call and make request to constantly borrow money should be treated like a business venture. Make them sign a letter stating that they will repay you, add $25.00 to the amount they are borrowing and then, if you have the money, give it to them but don't expect it to be given back.

REASON: Loaning money between friends and family will destroy the relationship and be that pimple on the nose hard to pop.

On the matter of "your business" keep it to yourself

Robin and Jenifer

No matter how deeply you trust some people outside of family, (and then again, some family members hold secrets like a mop bucket with 17 two-inch holes) keep a great deal of things close to the vest. Not all your personal happenings should be discussed openly to people who are your party friends, business associates and casual acquaintances. They will pass on deep secrets to other people, just like they do you with you when they are discussing other folk's business.

REASON: People will talk about you behind your back because jealousy and hatred run deep and silent in all of us. I just want you to have a higher standard of living than all your peers.

On the issue of looking your best

Society has its idea of how a woman should dress and what is acceptable. The idea of being sexy all of the time just doesn't resonate in all occasions and in at all events. Take care of how you look and make sure you dress for you and how you feel it will make you beautiful and strong throughout your day.

REASON: Dress for you. Dress as if you are going to win the world through the power you display in your beauty and your walk. Looking your best at all times should be the foundation for how you choose your wardrobe because you never know who will cross your path and if that one meeting may be someone who will be interviewing you for a potential job.

On the question of finding a good man

Virgil, Jr. and Terhea

Nesting is the age old standards that some parents used to teach their sons. In this mode, the boy prepares himself to become a responsible man. He completes his training, education and gets his credit score up to a solid level. He has two bank accounts—one for his bills and one for emergencies. Look for all of that in the guy you choose to replace me in your life.

REASON: You don't want a man that you either have to raise or take care of from the first days of your relationship and future.

Jacke and his daughter Corintha

On the issues of tipping a waiter or waitress

Robin, Cailyn, Melissa and Jaleesa

In your life you will have those days and nights where you will take time to go out and eat. The major item which will cause your dining experience to fall and falter from being perfect will be the actions of the wait staff. It took me a while to get past the attitudes and understand that they are people who have lives and are not receiving the monies they should for the work they do. Treat them with respect at every encounter—no matter if they are dry in their speech, rude in their delivery or late bringing the food to your table. People do make mistakes and have bad days. From my experience, when I have left tips for the "mean waitress" my next visits to that restaurant have always been pleasant. And we have had that same person wait on us—and their tip was increased because of it.

REASON: Find you a baseline amount that you will not go below when leaving a tip. I have found leaving $7.00 for the tip— even if the waitress / waiter has been less than subpar, allows you to be in the example of Christ Jesus by blessing someone who doesn't deserve any gift.

And if you think back on your days, you have been continually blessed and have the power to add some good into another person's day.

On the issue of dating and being "friends with benefits"

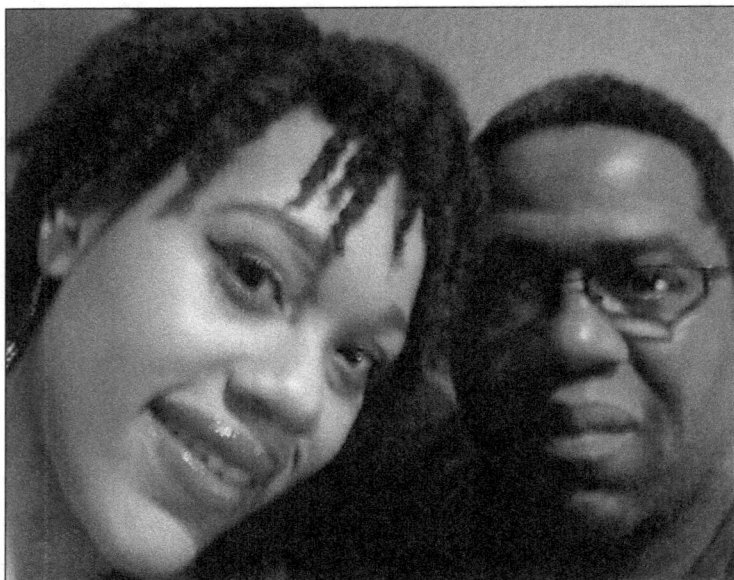

Robin and Amber Rae

Being in Love . . . don't fall in love until you trip over the foundations of friendship. I know how it feels to be in love and then to have that fall apart. Take your time to learn everything about the person you are giving your BEST to.

REASON: Their level of commitment may not be based on the same intensity as yours. And you don't want to share the feeling of love too early and never have it reciprocated.

On the question of being stressed and not talking

Mike and Kirvin

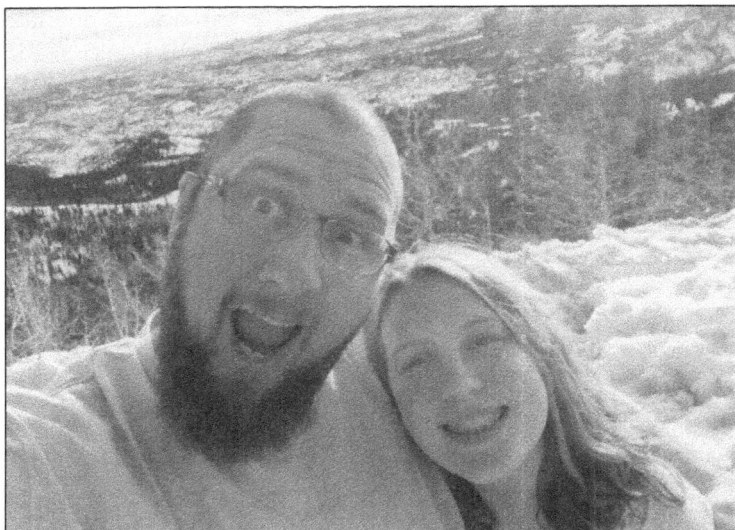

Dan and Piper

Being Alone . . . you are never alone. I am here to listen. There is no issue in this world where you have to fear talking to me. I may not like what I hear, but I will sit and work with you to get you to a place of peace.

REASON: I don't want you so stress and overwhelmed that you make quick and rash decisions based on emotions or pressure from other people. Let's talk about it and AT ANY TIME.

On the issue of becoming a greater person

Corey and Sariah

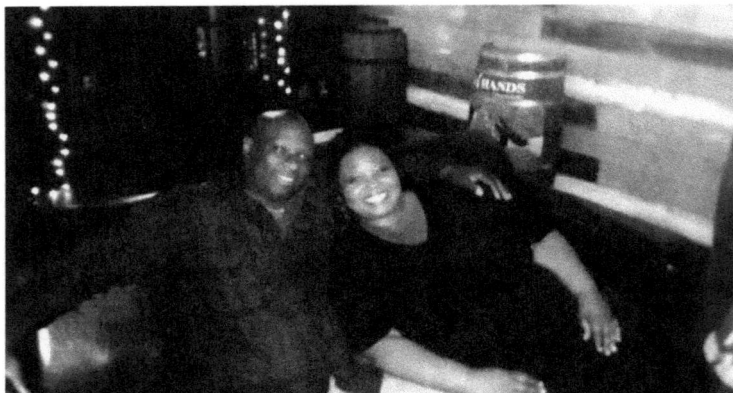

Greg and Melissa

Information and Education should be based on context. In order for you to hear the full conversation, remove what you know when engaging others people outside your normal context. This way you remove all those pre-placed barriers and nonsense added in you by those people you've known for years. Misinformation based on cultural biases will force you to miss out on some great human beings.

REASON: Take everyone you meet and know at face value. Take the time to listen to what they are always talking about and how they act / react around "other" people on a day to day basis. This will allow you to see how deep their humanity flows and how far you can be open with them.

On the issue of you becoming a great cook

William, III and Shenya

Cooking and Baking is a separate and unique job by itself. One thing I want you to do before you walk into the kitchen. Please use the bathroom before you begin cooking dinner for anyone. There may be those times when you have to poot and you are in the middle mixing. You don't need to mix that mess into the meals created for later. Especially when you mother is coming over to eat with you.

REASON: Take time to prepare all your meals with a prayerful heart and a determined mind. In this, most of your cooking endeavors will be a great tasting masterpiece.

On the matter of being private in your dealings
New Relationships

Robin's daughters—Chrishanda, Jesika and Amber

Do not tell your new boyfriend all of your dating history. This new person will ingest all that you say and unconsciously make plans and angles to try and look better than the previous guy. But will also remember all the things you've said in conversation of how the last person had taken advantage of you or make note of all the things you allowed to go on and how long it was before you put your foot down to end the frustration.

REASON: Don't base your new relationship on old baggage and hurts. If you are reminded of those old things, you've not healed and you and I need to have a dinner date and talk about how you can move forward.

On the issue of you driving
after 11:00 o'clock at night

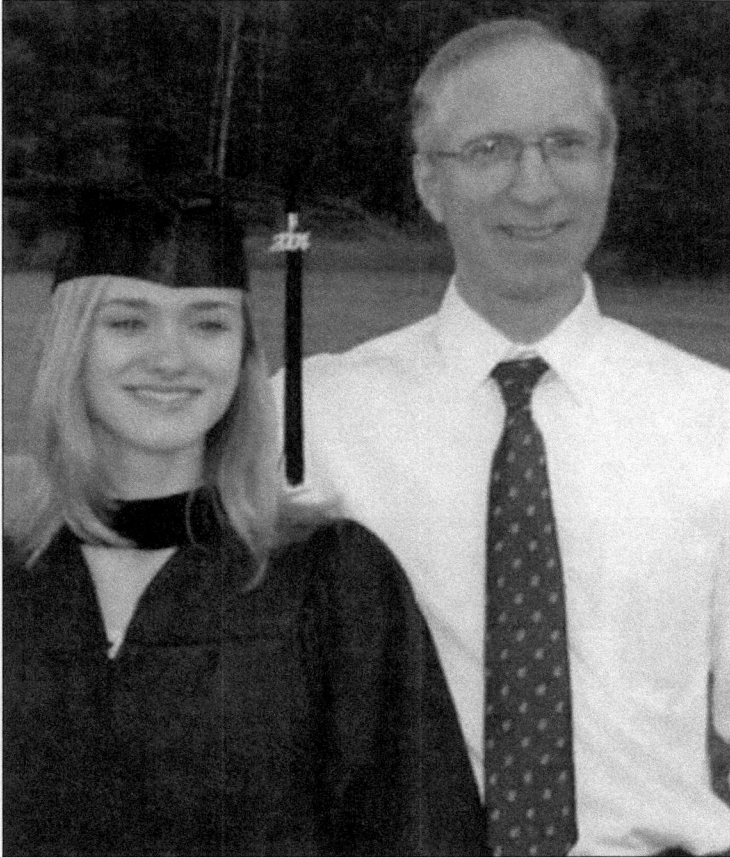

Stan and Sarah

Denis, Antonique and Amerie

If you are out and about after 11:00 o'clock and driving on the freeway, please drive in the slow lane. This is not to fuss at you for being out late and going party. The right lane will always be the safest lane at this time of night and traffic will not force you to make wrong decisions.

REASON: Drunk drivers tend to have drunk driving accidents going the wrong way on the freeway and will be in the fast lane on your side because they think it is the slow lane, but don't realize they are headed into oncoming traffic.

Robin, Rebekah and Mikkel

On the issue of you going to the mall or grocery store

Grady, Gabby and Saniah

Where you decide to park does matter. If you are going to find a good parking spot, consider not parking by a panel van (the ones with no windows on the side), any large trucks and in dark or secluded areas. Even if you have one or two friends with you. Consider your area when you exit your car. Look around and take notice of who and what is around you. If you have a need to go to the store after 10:00 o'clock at night—let that desire ride until the next morning.

REASON: I don't want you to be assaulted by anyone in the parking lot or become the subject of a carjacking.

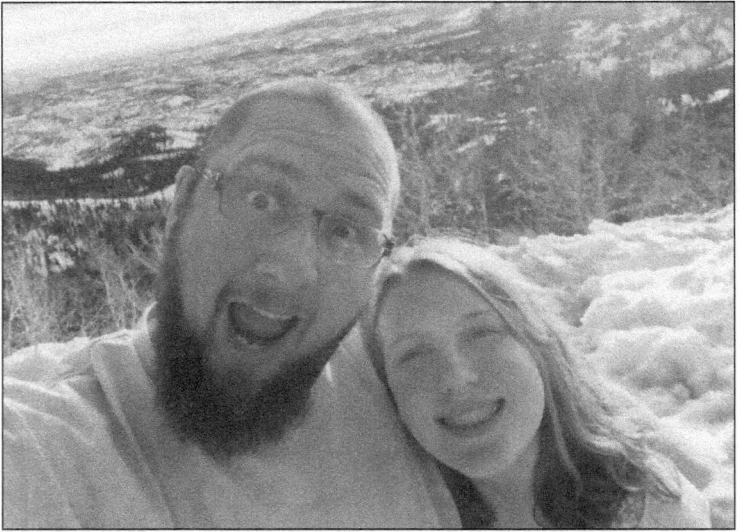

Dan and Piper

On the issue of having plugged bathroom pipes . . .

Chad and Riley

I know you are gonna say, "dad, that is just to gross to talk to you about!" But here it goes any way.

If you are in the bathroom and putting the kids in the pool, really consider the things I have always said to you, "Drop one, Flush one" It wasn't to be nasty or make you feel uncomfortable. It is to have the minimum times that you have to use the plunger and I have had to go in the bathroom and see you pooh plugging the bottom of the toilet.

REASON: Drop one; Flush one will allow you to kill off some of the horrendous odors that are emitted from the human body at that time and keeps the pipes clear and flowing.

On the issue of being friendly and remaining friendly . . .

Mike and Kirvin

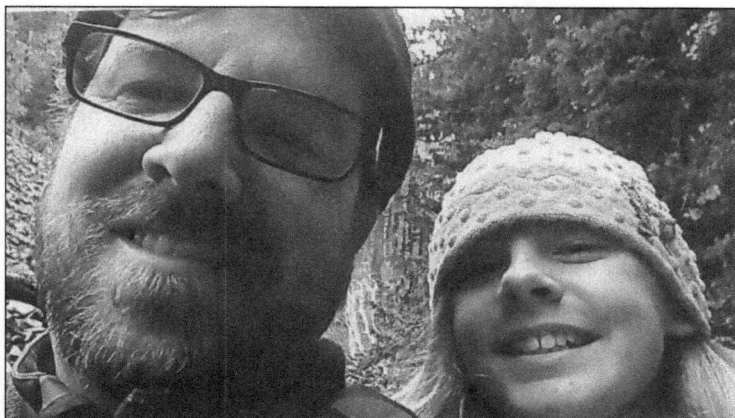

Mike and Kirvin

Sometimes there are those days that you just don't want to be bothered by certain people or you may have had a fallen out with one of your girlfriends, don't shut the door. It is okay to be away from people for a good period. This will allow you and that person time to cool off.

Even in the moment of a heated discussion, take the time to take a breath before you respond. Count 1001 and 10002 before you utter one word. If you cannot keep from blowing up and losing your cool and breaking that perfect persona I know you have, just walk away.

REASON: it is far better to have a friend in the wings than not to have someone to call on when you just need to hear some good advice or have a laugh at an old joke or memory. And then again, you might have some concert tickets and need a 3rd wheel because the guy just isn't worth being alone with (I am just saying)

On the issues of your RISING UP from a letdown in your day . . .

There will be those days in which it seems that all things have broken down so much that you're the chapter in your story can destroy your image. I would like you understand that the negatives that can and will happen cannot define you and give you the decision to give up and quit. Rising up will be that mixture of you taking the negatives and integrating them into all the positives which make you the great person you are.

REASON: The pause that you need to take in your day has to be that day when you rework your plans to change the next chapter. After a breakup, letdown and loss of job, realize that the strength in you comes, not from me or your mother, but from the brilliance and strength that is within you. You have the ability to adjust and keep on moving.

Missing Church? Not a Problem

I want you to be protected all the days of your life. So those Sundays when you do not make it to church service or you are feeling low in spirit, I have placed some inspirational messages to get you through your rough patches and keep you in touch with God.

I got them from the book, *CONSIDER THIS ON THIS DAY*. I hope you will take a few minutes and read them.

Consider On This Day: becoming the SUPER woman you should be . . . and should realize is already alive . . .

In the search for a good life, we sometimes tend to sell ourselves short of all the talents given. In particular, women are given a tower of strength, which has been pushed down to what she may wear, how it fits on her, what size she may be and if she is sexy enough to be on a guy's arm (if he takes her out).

God has made a woman to be the "Help Meet" of the man He has created for her.

The problem in becoming that SUPER woman . . . some settle for the first thing breathing and are angry, upset, disappointed, discouraged, disgusted and empty at the end of most days. And then the long days of not believing in their talents are if they have reached their true purpose and potential and did not know it.

The fact of the matter is this, IT IS MORE THAN OKAY TO BE SINGLE FOR A WHILE . . . there is not a man on this earth worth the salt in your tears, if he is not willing to lift you up on a daily basis, thank you for listening to him cry about nothing on most days and a few good things on the 12 really bad days that may cause him to want to give up.

. . . there is not any one person, who should rule over how YOU believe and think about yourself. Your self-worth is in the Hands of God and you have been blessed before you realize what you have and who you truly are . . . you do not need one single person to validate what has already been ordained from above . . . YOU were created to do super things through tough and trying times.

Most psychologists state that women are too emotional and cannot handle stressful situations and keep their self-esteem and self-efficacy intact . . . spit on that and keep pushing on as you have been doing. You have made it this far in life

To solidify your daily strength . . . read Psalms 40 & 43 . . . there is Grace and Favor that are waiting for you and the Hope that we all have in knowing that God will not leave you in a void and unprofitable situation or heated circumstances . . . it is your choice to be the "wifey or the superwoman" . . . choose this day where truly want to remain and be known as.

Ladies, in Proverbs 31, it speaks of the Woman that is behind the man. The Word shows how strong her character are and who benefits from her being that strong rock and tower for her husband.

In being the backbone of that man, your actions cannot mirror his or cause him to stumble and fall. If you are his and he is truly acting as yours . . . be his . . . talk openly with him (not to / at him) tell him those things that you wish to obtain and how you want to be treated. Respect and Honor only arrive when the when the entire house is clean . . . both of you having to talk to one another . . . openly . . . And all things spoken have to remain between You and He (no boys or my girl's thang). This is a couple's thing that turns two into one . . . that is spiritually based.

But if you are single, love yourself and learn of yourself, before meeting that new person. It is okay to be single in a world of broken-barely working relationships and half-promised/half-married couples. Be true to you and believe in all the things that have been given you by God.

Consider On This Day: The Object of Love

We all have heard the stories of falling in love, being in love and falling out of love.

We all understand the degrees of love to one extent or another.

We have heard the use of love over run, over explained and over used in churches for us to extend or fill the coffers of tithe and offering (I Corinthians 13) . . .. but those are used in the wrong context and hinder God's blessings for His children (this will be explained on another date because Benevolence Offering is man-made).

The powers of love can either cause us to move immediately or give up our last to make a friend or family member's circumstance less painful. We would rather have the burden of another put on our shoulders, rather than have them suffer too long and get the understanding or lesson from making bad decisions.

Looking at the changes in life, we can see that all things can either be a blessing or another lesson learned.

The three degrees of love are as follows:

1. Agape—Unconditional . . . Undying

Most of us try to equate this type of love only to a Godly nature

2. Philae—Conditional . . . Discriminating . . . Limited in Nature . . . Fails

Most of us have experienced this is varying relationships

3. Eros—Emotional and Purely Sense Driven . . . based more on physical traits

All of us have given into the physical desires of the flesh—we fell in love because it hurt not to be around that certain person

Ex: A woman meets a man (man meets a woman) . . . they fall in love . . . this is based on physical traits and desires . . . this is what he looks like, what he can offer, if he can rock her world, what job he holds, how he looks, what he drives . . . In the man's case—he is more physical than she . . . he considers the list and also adds . . . is she going make my boys jealous . . . is she going to make me look good in public . . . and will she be easy enough to control . . . these things are taking into consideration on some level(this is Eros). The relationship may last for a period of time, well until it is time for the relationship to move into the next phase . . . becoming friends . . . yes . . . friends . . . the order is mixed up because we do not seek to learn the person before becoming physical—so the relationship is EROS for too long.

The Phileo stage . . . the woman needs someone to talk to . . . she doesn't talk to him . . . well . . . he does not understand because the deepest parts of him in this relationship is stuck in EROS . . . and when things and circumstances hit the fan . . . AGAPE . . . does not have a stronghold . . . the relationship started in the wrong order and the PHILEO never grows so the woman and man hit the pavement again in search of a new LOVE . . . because neither person is willing to give unless they are getting something in return . . . Phileo not Agape

The object of love is not based on how "Godly" we can act, but how strong a fellowship is between individuals when dealing with one another. No one person can say that they have not experienced all three types and walked away and not been changed in some form or fashion. When objectively looking at Christ, He experienced all of these degrees of love towards us. His base actions in deciding to fulfill the prophecy of the Gospel have us at this point today. Now we all know that the Gospel is this: The Death, Burial and Resurrection . . . anything added to this is a falsehood.

His actions toward us was Eros . . . because He saw that our physical nature would always stand in the way of a good fellowship with the Father . . . we always want to do good and cannot, because we are easily distracted.

His actions toward us were Phileo . . . His relationship with us was on one level, when it needed to be much much more . . . the plan started with the Jews and was extended to all of us

His actions toward us is Agape . . . there was no condition that stood in the way of His love for us and the actions that were needed to seal us into Everlasting

His order was completely correct . . . He loved us before WE knew of Him . . . this is in His covenant with Abraham . . . all of His actions in dealing with the Israelites . . . all of His actions in touching Paul on the Damascus road . . . He loved us through Calvary . . . He loves us enough to let us keep lying to Him, putting things off that will get us closer to Him . . . Putting things off that would make the peace in our homes stronger and longer lasting . . . Putting things off that would allow us not to be so selfish to the people who live under the same roof with us . . . He loves us more than we can think of or understand . . . He loves us Unconditionally—Agape . . . He loves us better than our own spouses, children and brothers and sister—Phileo . . . He loved us until it hurt HIM . . . Eros . . . He loved us all the way to His death and rising . . . He loves us even when we look in the mirror and question the reasons for us being who we are and wonder why He has not moved in our lives like we want Him to . . .

Some may feel a need to get upset and not see that Christ had to feel all degrees of love for us in order to understand HOW SORRY WE TRULY ARE ON A DAY TO DAY BASIS.

His love in our lives is limited because we live limited lives . . . based on the limitations of what we want to give out . . . knowing that the more we give to Him . . . the more we shall receive from Him. The problems that we all have in our homes, in some degree is founded in the way we react to, talk to, understand, and LOVE one another . . . open that door on this day . . . okay?? Fellowship (talk) to him/her today.

***Mark 12:31 and the second is like, namely this, thou shall love thy neighbor as thyself. There is none other commandment greater than these.

Consider On This Day: Talk is Cheap and Does Not Need Repeating

The problem with dirt . . . Most would think that if they would talk about a person or bring up their past repeatedly, it would cause harm, tear up your day, stop you from moving away from them, end the pointless relationship, break you down, force you to quit and give up and make you stumble back into the old you . . .

BUT there is one thing to understand about dirt . . . the more it is tilled, turned over, cultivated, pruned of trash and debris, broken apart and a loosened; the better air and water can get to the through.

It is those tough things that that we all must go through, which teaches us lessons and strengthens our resolve and relationship with God when and while no one else wants to hear our pleas and tears. God sees our tears and knows what we should become . . . in spite of our past . . .

It is those tough things which allow us to drop a tear, and then realize that those friends who use our failures and faults to prop themselves up to be better people than us can be just like a leaf on a pear tree in the winter time—gone for good. Let them talk themselves out of a good friendship.

Think on this

When one is working in a garden, the first thing which has to be done; it the breaking up of old ground and rocks and soil. This is what Jesus does in our lives when we ask for certain blessings and gifts . . . our days and lives have to be prepared for the seeds of good fruit to be planted.

In the book of Isa. 28:24, the question is asked—Does the plowman plow all day to sow? Does he open and break the clods of his ground? The problem with the Plowman is that he has no concern of what comes behind him. He is just there to break up the old stuff. There is not a thought to what is to become of the tilled and turned over dirt.

But is the Plowman and our friends and friend-enemies would realize—is that the more they turn over and till our dirt, the better we become in this world.

We serve an awesome God

We serve a God that keeps giving us—chance after chance after change after change after chance after change after chance . . . and before you know it . . . we are not the same person that we once were. We somehow have a better understanding of the 3rd chapter of the book of James

We somehow can just shake off the dust and dirt thrown at us by the people who are supposed to love and care for us

How can a man (or woman) speak of love to you and call you names and use words he would not use to his own dog? And you love him back?

Start believing in your own talents and stop waiting for validation from a "selfish fool".

We somehow can look back at the fields of our lives and truly say, "how did this happen and how did I get over?"

So on this day . . . take this scripture with you . . .

"Sow to yourselves in righteousness, reap in mercy; break up your fallow ground: for it is time to seek the LORD, till he come and rain righteousness upon you."

Let them talk . . . Let them talk . . . Let them talk . . . Let them talk . . . Let them break up the ground that you are unable to look at or talk about . . . BUT when they do . . . speak the Word over your life . . . Speak positive and great things into the days of your children, your spouse, your brothers and your sisters . . . Speak over yourself and wait for the God of another chance to make the great changes in your life . . . Let them talk and point fingers . . . Let them stay busy looking at piles of dirt—While you walk on with the blessings of good fruit.

It is He that will come behind the Plowman and adds increase into fields that are said to be bitter, useless and barren. God has made us to be the head and not the tail . . . stop accepting everything people say about you as if it were the Gospel . . . Speak over yourself those things that you have prayed into your life . . . Speak great things into your days . . . stop repeating what they have said about you as if it were true . . . Speak great things into your days because God did not make you to be anyone's footstool or mat.

You are a Child of the King . . . So act like royalty . . . Speak like the royal you truly are.

Speak the Word over your house, over your car, over your job, over your children and in all your days!
Speak great things into your day if no one else will.

Realize this, all things in your life begin with how you feel and think about yourself.

Consider On This Day: Me, Arrogant?

In our many days on this Earth, we have experienced a great deal of trials, setbacks, hurts and pains. But after going through all of this, we are still standing and sometimes a little attitude has assisted us along the way.

Arrogance is defined as having an attitude of superiority, manifested within an overbearing manner or in presumptuous claims or assumptions.

I am taking this tag as a compliment, based on all those things God has allowed me to get over, go through, be on top of, leave behind and folk I have walked away from—because I did not act like them any longer.

There should be this understanding that when someone/anyone comes in contact with the Saving Power of Jesus the Christ . . . we can no longer be the same. In Romans 8, the Bible tells us that those who are in contact with Christ and have gone through and arrived—Well, we are more than conquerors

- Some of us have walked away from an addiction to drugs and alcohol
- Some of us have walked away from a life of lying and cheating
- Some of us have walked away from days and nights of being used and abused by people

So if we have an attitude, it is an attitude that WE WILL NOT BE HELD DOWN ANY LONGER.

If you cannot stand the power of my praise . . . stand back

stand back in awe and watch Christ continue to work and our light shine brighter

stand back and see me be the one in the crowd others look at

stand back and watch the devil run from me because of Who's I AM

Yes, I am arrogant

Yes, I have an attitude

I have an attitude because I am saved and I am filled with the power granted me by God

Read Psalms 150

Consider On This Day: They Just Don't Get It

It has been often said, "Experience is the best teacher", and I do believe this to be a fact in all of my days.

Some of our days may seem as if we are trekking uphill on a rainy day, we still find footing and make it to the top of the hill; stronger and wiser than when those days began. Then there are those days, where the sun is so bright and the skies are clear that we step strong and hard, but are leery for the change of wind.

All of the things and people we have experienced gives us enough pause to stop and call on the Lord on a moment's notice; if not audible—our hearts speak the Word into every situation.

Then comes the questions from those who are around us and they ask, "How did you not cuss that fool out?" or "Why did you not just give up and quit?"

Described in I Peter 2 is the changes and the reasons behind those changes which have taken place in us which answer the questions above. The process of salvation is a slow and permanent one. It is so slow, that the people around us ridicule, cuss and then make comments that would cause us to almost join in with them when it seems all the walls are closing in on our lives. But then there is the Holy Spirit reminding us of the gift which has separated us from that "old man" we used to be.

Some people just don't get the change in us. They expect us to attend church, but remain focused on the falling rain as if we cannot find solid ground in all of life's muddy places.

Some people don't get it because they choose not to accept the level of maturity that comes with experiencing life through the saving grace of God. They want us to act out of turn and not be who God has called us to become.

Yes, this is a process! A process that moves us to become that question in the lives of all the people who know us and know about us. We become that question, which causes those who don't get to see Christ Jesus in all of our actions and forces them to hear our living testimony every time they approach us and ask, "What is the reason behind your focus in life?"

God has called us to be better than the average person. He has separated us to be that force of change in the circle of influence for our friends and family. No matter how much we are liked or not liked—they will see Jesus in us. That is—if our testimony matches all of our actions.

They don't get it on a daily basis, but they do see it—because most Christians don't half step into their blessings.

READ I Peter 2:1–9

Consider On This Day: The Times Are Decision Breakers / Makers

Inopportune Times . . . can be defined as inappropriately timed or made from bad decisions

As we know the timing on some things arrive at the right moment, when we absolutely need them. They hit on the right number in the day and save us from weeks of grief and stress.

The money came in on time . . .

What is upsetting are those times, when the opportunity to say some things does not quite match up and the situation spirals out of control.

We have all had little fusses, tiffs, arguments and disagreements and allowed those things that we know would hurt, destroy or steal the outcome of that little tiff to be a victory for us . . . to slip from our lips.

And in these times, we look for God to still be on our side, when we know that the Holy Spirit has been with us each and every time that we have . . . thought on, lied on, moved to get back at some on, said the wrong things to the wrong people—just to hurt them—because we were mad at them at one time, went on the creep for a one night stand (didn't say you did it, but it is the same thing—wrong), held money back from our bills and asked our spouse to cover the rest—just to have a few dollars in hand Well, those things are all grieving the Holy Spirit.

Those simple things are the base reasons why we do not receive our blessings on TIME.

If we would only use a little common sense and patience after we have asked God to relieve our stressful times.

If we would just take a moment to think, while in the midst of a heated discussion, we would realize that those things which are said—HAVE NO DIRECT BEARING on the real situation needed to be discussed.

If we would openly communicate with the person we say we love—then there would not be a reason to look upon another for tenderness and affection—cheating is not genetic . . . it is a decision ill-timed.

If we would only trust God for the change and stop trying to steal from the blessings He has given to us His efforts to teach us how to handle bigger and larger blessings . . . our days and lives would be so much better.

If we would only apologize for those wrong things that we have said to the people we love . . . the spirit of love will move a great deal easier in our days . . . right???

Our days are filled with opportunities to not only be blessed, but bless others

Those things that we are holding onto in the closet—will not grow two sizes because you loved wearing it at one time or another . . . There are those organizations that would love to grant those things to others, who do not have adequate dress to look for work or go to church . . . make a donation . . . make room in your life and heart so that you can be able to receive other blessings on TIME.

Consider On This Day: Validation and Affirmation

Sitting back and thinking over your life is one thing. To walk back through all the memories can sometimes be a difficult journey.

In both, the task is all about choices and a desire to inspect those areas in which some bad and not so great choices were made. Realization comes when we look at all the times we have fallen but understand that we are better for trying to do some things, while failing at others. But we are still standing. We are all the better for having travelled some roads.

We are validated through the decisions made which caused us to take pause and grow. We are validated because we know and understand where we came from and the reasons behind the strength we now use to get through familiar storms.

In the 3rd chapter of Philippians, the Apostle Paul takes pen in hand and tells his story and why he can stand in the midst of being imprisoned, ridiculed and facing being ostracized or killed by the Roman Government. Paul takes the time to list out all the areas of his heritage that makes him stronger, but then makes a sharp turn to let us know that without Christ our lives can never be affirmed, nor reach the places we were created to walk.

Nothing in life is either simple or easy. If all things were simple and easy, we'd never learn a thing or amount to the persons we should become in the first place.

Example

If a husband never takes five minutes out of his day to tell his wife that she is beautiful and smart, there will be that one guy who is always waiting for the opportunity to whisper to her those things the husband never validates. The wife's affirmation will be gifted by someone who only wants to control her for a few moments.

If a mother never takes the time to teach her son the value of a hug and a kiss on the cheek, and then require him to be a gentleman and open the door for her, he will not be able to appreciate the love of a good woman, nor understand that it is within his power to create space enough for his wife and daughters to mature into the powerful creatures they were designed to be.

If a father routinely neglects to tell his daughter that she is a champion, an overcomer and talented, and speaks kind and loving words into her days, then she will never understand the reasons why a good man should never raise his hands and strike her and call her out of her name—regardless the situation.

The lines of nurturing and loving start early and should never be retired or redrawn. Our movement toward our families must be in the example of Christ Jesus. We must be willing to tell all and give all for those we love and cherish to become better than we ever could be.

Paul's message to the Philippians wasn't designed to bolster any of his achievements, but allow an understanding to surface that will show the world that no matter the greatest things accomplished, there is not one thing on this earth which can outlast, out give or out-perform the love Christ Jesus has for His church.

Read: Philippians 3:4–14

make this day the day you look at all the things in your past and count it all joy because you have made it through the rough times and you are now standing long after you'd thought of giving up and giving in.

Consider On This Day: The Weight or to Wait

Hebrews 12:1—Wherefore seeing we also are compassed about with so great a cloud of witnesses, let us lay aside every weight, and the sin which doth so easily beset us, and let us run with patience the race that is set before us . . .

Our days are filled with the transitions of pain, suffering, arguments, failed relationships, bad ideas and some good ideas. It is the times in between all of this which causes us to consider making bad decisions in the midst of changes . . . we want to rush the outcome to fit what we think are beneficial for the circumstances we face. It is the weight of trying to overcome stresses and tragedy that presses us to make immediate decisions.

If we would start all our days as a family and give those days to God . . . will this make the days better or brighter??

If we would take the time to sit down and think on the things that we have accomplished, search the scriptures or history to see what more successful people have done to get over similar situations . . . we would see that the witness that their accomplishments will allow us to make bettered decisions and possibly teach us to wait . . . this would mean growing patience in our lives and our days.

THOUGH the pressures of life may be pushing us to make a yes or no decision . . . It is always the ability to wait on change . . . that we all have inside of us which will allow us to see that slow change is more permanent than a quick fix. Waiting one more hour . . . Waiting one more day . . . Waiting one more week . . . will allow for more contemplation on the subject matter and more time to pray on it . . . why rush to an end, when the entire situational end may take 30 days or more??

(Psalms 27:14 Wait on the LORD: be of good courage, and he shall strengthen thine heart: wait, I say, on the LORD.)

Consider On This Day: Situation and Circumstance

Situation is defined as this: a controlled or designed plan of action, a set pattern of events or a state of affairs.

On the other hand . . .

Circumstance is defined as this: the result of or sum of un-calculated, unplanned and unwarranted factors beyond willful human control.

The events of our day are always a type of learning curve for most of us. Some things we gain and others we lose. Those events, good or bad; both teach us to grow and train us toward a point of maturity allowing us to become better persons, parents, friends and Children of God. We often make steps in situations—knowing that the decisions we make will have a serious impact on our days and weeks to come. BUT sometimes . . . we step into situations knowing that the circumstances from them will be dire and hard on us and the people in our lives . . . BUT . . . we still try to make bad situations end up with good outcomes. We end up losing a great deal more than we bargained for or thought would take place.

The choice is always doing we choose what is good or do we choose what is knowingly bad

example:

Situation: A deeply educated, well-respected, friendly wom-an—knows a good looking and popular street-smart man. She knows and understands that in the past three years he has not held a job more than two solids months at a time. He has lived with several women and could possibly have several children that he does not act as a father towards. She pursues him and becomes involved with him. They say they love each other.

Circumstance: Since she has gotten with him . . . she has not driven her own car in weeks . . . she is always late for work, her house always has other folk in it when he is there or not, her ap-pearance has gone from "put together' to just making it, she has to constantly be on the lookout for the angry EX-Girlfriend and she does not spend time with her family and friends as before.

The Answer

Proverbs 3:5–6—tells us to "Trust in the Lord with all of our heart and lean not toward our own understanding and in ALL our ways acknowledge Him . . .

Matthew 6:33—tells us to "Seek the kingdom of God first and all things will be added to our days and our lives.

In understanding any situation, if we are to be successful on a daily basis, we should put Christ first in the plans of what, who and why we move. It is when the opportunities arise that we think we are more than what we truly are and what we truly understand and know. NO—this woman could not save this man nor was he the man that God created for her . . . the same situation for the man . . . just because someone looks good and all things around them seem to shine, that person may not be the GIFT that God has created for you to advance further in life. . . . . . .and the outcome will always be that we lose our homes, cars, money, jobs and ourselves behind people and things that we want to make right in our pursuit of the best situation.

Consider your choices and talk to God for the best answer possible.

Consider On This Day: Throw Caution to the Wind

Facing a new day brings about those who will tell others how and when they can let go and release all things to God. This is just a bunch of nonsense. Certain titles and length of time worshipping in a certain place does not usher in any kind of authority over the Holy Spirit or how and when one can open up and praise God.

Be excited about today. Go for a walk and take in all of creation and be excited that you are still alive to appreciate it all

Psalms 100 & 150 tells all of creation to praise and worship the Creator with all the power that resides in our beating hearts.

Consider On This Day: Standards Are Important

A standard is simply defined as a set of rules which ensure quality in all areas.

In this life we look to achieve and complete certain things in our pursuit of happiness. The joy which receive each morning is a blessing bestowed on us by Grace and Mercy . . . The trials that we find ourselves during the passing of time in each of our days, both try our patience and intelligence and we then have to make choices on what we should do.

In this, we either choose to follow what we know is correct and right or we take the easiest road and go against our morals and the ideals which make us known as good people and children of God. We go against the standards our parents put in us and the standards that we choose to pursue in our quest to be better individuals, parents and friends.

Example

In any high school—we fall under the mascot and the school's standard. We act a certain way and believe that the set standards of that school are the best in the land . . . no one school is better than the one we graduated from—because of the standards which are set as the foundation of that school. We march under that flag with big smiles on our faces. As a country we follow a certain flag and are expected to carry ourselves as Americans and be proud of the fact that we are Americans . . . so we hold to that standard and ideal

As Christians—As Children of God . . . our standards should be unshakeable, unmovable. But in order to satisfy our friends and the people WE choose to have in our lives—we lower the standards which we know our parents set in us, the standards we received in school and the standards God has instilled in our souls and we make bad choices and do not pray on those choices until the situations and circumstances are out of control . . . God calls us to be better in all areas of our lives. This is not just for ourselves, but for the people in our circle of influence . . . if we start doing better

and acting better and making better choices . . . our friends and associates and partners will see that change in us and strive to reach
greater heights in this life . . . and this may persuade our children
to become better adults than we are ------having greater standards.
But marching under this flag, many days we don't smile, but hides
our pride and praise from and about the blessings we receive from
Him due to His standards . . . marching under His flag changes a
great many people.

Let's change the next generation by raising the standards of
our days.

Read the book of Joshua—chapters one and two.

Consider On This Day: Am I Who I Pretend to Be

The choices we make daily have a direct effect upon us and our children's blessings and future.

The image we know of ourselves and then give out in the daily grind can be two separate people.

That is a struggle within itself.

Our children and family know how we fake things to the world. They see that fight and struggle. We have to work each moment and seek to become the person God created us to be. This may not please our old friends and lovers, but it the daily call for us to live and move at a higher standard in life.

Why give our children and family the short end on the stick when we know we can be and do better?

Why live in mediocrity when the talents we possess calls for a small effort?

In Romans 6:1, Paul speaks of the baptism and how God's children are SUPPOSED to act after the spiritual acceptance of Christ and the physical dip / dunk in the water. We all are to walk in a higher standard of life.

The question is constantly asked about and our fellowship in Christ, 'are they really who they say they are?' Let them keep asking while you make the decision to allow God to direct you into a better lifestyle and better friends. Friends who will work with you about your growing stronger in the daily grind and not beat you down.

We can understand if bad choices made while acting like a Christian gives out negative answers, which is on us and shows badly upon our children and the church. Strong decisions must be made daily in the attempt to fight off the enemy and keep our name strong and in the light.

READ Romans 6th chapter.

make this day the day you open up and allow His Spirit to evaluate and change you—totally.

Consider On This Day: What Type of Friends Do You Really Have?

Sometimes those things that we hold dear in life could possibly be that one major drawback or hurdle stopping us from getting ahead, overcoming, realizing our goals, grasping our dreams and becoming the great person that we had been destined to be all along. Or friends have the most influence in and over our lives outside the Hands of God.

In Proverbs 17:17. . . "A friend loveth at all times, and a brother is born for adversity" . . . Stating that we only rely on our siblings for so long. Our siblings know our shortcomings and faults and will use them to speak and talk us out of some of the things that are needed in better our OWN families outside of what our mothers and fathers had given birth. This is called sibling rivalry. They will help us for so long and so far . . . but when we call on our friends— well that is a different story

And being the social animals we are, we need friends to assist us in finding out how strong, dependable and reasonable we really can and will be. Proverbs 18:24 states that "a man that hath friends must show himself friendly: and there is a friend that sticketh closer than a brother".

There are four types of friends to consider:

The Finger Bone

The Funny Bone

The Hip Bone

The Back Bone

The Finger Bone friend is someone who seems to have it all together, but the only thing they do is try to point in the direction of . . . "If it were me, I would take that job. I am just saying" or "if I were you, I wouldn't go back to school right now. You know how much time that will take for you to finish that degree? I am just saying." And the entire time, they are not working, they always need to hold some of your money and they never have a stable relationship . . . and their advice is always THE BEST.

They are like fingers—they can only point you in the direction that you should go . . . ...Because they themselves are unable to take the necessary steps to better their own lives.

The Funny Bone friend is someone who has had several jobs in the last five years. Always can find a job, but keeping one is truly a different story. They do not take life to serious right now. They say that they are too young and life is way too short to focus on the future right now.

THEY HAVE BEEN SAYING THAT FOR YEARS.

They owe you money. They always want to ride in your car. They always can find the spot and the party to spend your money and burn your gas. Let things get hard in your life and you cannot find them. They have no plans on helping you, because they do not possess the capabilities or talents to help themselves. Every time you ask about your money or to ride in their car—a joke comes out of their mouths to divert the conversation

They are like the elbow. They will bend and change the shape of your life, but nothing can be gifted from them because they lack the mindset to create, grasp and maintain the talents to hit the ground and work—they are hit with a situation and they find it funny because they have a feeling.

The Hip Bone Friend is a friend that seems to be in the right place at the right time. They have held the same job and position for quite some time. They keep a relationship going, but never get real serious. They are there when you call, but cannot give you real advice—they tell you to call someone else to see if they are right and correct. They will take steps with you, while you work hard and make ends meet, but they always seem to get out of all situations, those things which will benefit them.

They are like hips . . . they are with you and sway and shake as long as you are taking those steps to make something of yourself.

The Back Bone Friend is that one person who does not call on you all of the time, but when things seem to fall apart in your life . . . they show up, they call or they text at the exact time to not only offer advice or a way out, but offer themselves to you to assist you in carrying your burden. You know these folk. They have gotten and keep getting better in life. We tend not to hang around them because they are goal oriented and would like to pull us up to their level.

They are like the back bone . . . you do not think of them, but they always have your back and will pack you around and only complain when the load you are carrying is not truly the weight you should have in your life.

The power of friendship is a strong motivator in this life. The way to become better and obtain those things which are needed in succeeding in this life and get out of the inherited cycle of our great grandparents, grandparents, mothers and fathers is to change our Circle of Influence. We have to find those friends and associates who are getting it done. We have to take notes on those things they use to get better and incorporate them into us and our children in order to overcome the deep burdens of this world.

*Pray, make a 3-year plan on getting on your feet, pray and then drop those friends who have become anchors and roadblocks in all of your days . . . even if you have known them since grade school. You have to let go of your childhood at some time and be the adult you should become, right?

Consider On This Day: Going At It Alone

But there are those people who know us, walk with us, cry with us and get angry at the same things we do. These are the people that we enjoy having around. These are the people that inspire us to do better and reach for higher goals.

If the choice has been made to follow Christ and all the examples He has left, then GOOD friends are attribute that should be acquired and cherished. In Matthew 8, he speaks of the fellowship of GOOD friends being a benefit when all know Christ and are open to make request based on the need of the friend, the pain of a loved one and the need of the family and church and the whole time directing all things to God and not dishing out dirt on any subject. These actions allow you to see the power of God within His children and then in yourself.

United Prayer is the catalyst that will change habits, behaviors and the foundation of personal faith. Good company does not corrupt good morals, it strengthens them.

Yes, the Word does make it known that the devil is like a lion . . . seeking who he can destroy. The Word does not tell us that the devil is seeking a group of people, but that one person that will try to do things on their own and out of the strength of the fellowship. Yeah, I paraphrased . . . but there are only certain instances that individual success can be achieved and that success is only for that person. But when there is success by a group, it not only grows the power of the group . . . it makes all around stand up and take notice and then join into the group ----adding strength to the group.

I do know that we have friends and associates that are known from childhood. At some point in time, the idea of a childhood friend has to be dropped because we no longer are dealing with child-like issues. The enemy would like us ignorant and looking backwards. There is no growth in the future if the only thing thought about is recess, playgrounds, 8th grade dances, old high school loves and things left in the halls of a school you never return to.

This makes you distracted.

This makes you a target.

The devil may at times attack, but his attack fails when each person in the group remembers WHO is in the center of the group and WHO is the power source that allows the group to move as one. It is the familial draw of the group which gives singular focus to the problem and the solution.

Sometimes.

Sometimes.

Friends from the past that offer no positive incentive in your future MUST be left to be exactly what they are PAST FRIENDS. It is time for you to link up with stronger people to acquire and obtain those things God has gifted to you and your family . . . old friends can say hello to you at the class reunion and then you can tell them how good God has been to you

Make this the day that you open up and trust God to put GOOD people in your days that will inspire, encourage and push you to reach your full potential.

Consider On This Day: Running for Nothing

These are those days in our lives that we must move with distinct purpose and determination.

God has granted us with certain talents and gifts so we can be successful in this life, while living the example of being that SALT around our friends and family.

The race we are on is ours specifically. Not one single person can take any steps for us, breathe for us or sweat for us. This is our race alone. Whether the burden we are carrying is the load of issues covered with depression, anger, bouts of loneliness, gluttony, issues with sex and lies; it is ours alone to carry. It is ours alone to carry when we feel that we cannot make it to the next minute, next hour, next day or the next month . . . YOU have made it. And you have made it because you have been granted those certain talents and gifts to run your race at your pace. Not one person can take away the blessing that God has placed at the top of your hill and your mountain.

On this day, face your mountain and climb it or run up that single path that you know God has called you to follow. Run that path with the power that only you can feel that is being poured into you by God and God alone. A friend's advice is fine, but it is just advice. You take that advice and how you feel about yourself and bring it to God in the midst of running up your hill and listen for his direction on how to take your next step, your next breath, your next hurdle, your next detour.

You are not weak, you are not a sorry person, and you are not the failure others may call you or cause you to think. YOU are a Conqueror in Christ Jesus

Run . . . Run because you have the power to achieve all that is in you

Run . . . Run because you have made it passed half way and need to see things through

Run . . . Run because you need to be the SALT and prove all haters wrong

Run . . . Run because you have been blessed to endure your race to the end

Run . . . Run because not one person can detour or deter you from you appointed goal

READ 1 Corinthians 9:22—27

Consider On This Day: But God

Hounded and attacked from every side, beat down, lied on and lied to and confused on whom to turn to and trust in those dark and tearful times . . .

BUT GOD . . .

Tripped and stumbling through broken relationships and cheated on by a supposed faithful spouse and lover and given more lies to cover up the pain and embarrassment BUT GOD . . .

Psalm 57 explains that God takes His promises as serious as a Believer would take life itself. He will never turn, walk away and leave His children to suffer to the point they cannot get through the darkest of days. The psalmist begins by telling God that good friends and enemies work in unison to end him and his bid to be right in the eyesight and fellowship with God. And he reaffirms his belief that he can be rescued out all situations if he waits on God.

Can you wait on God's deliverance?

As I said on yesterday, you can either look for a stronger future by taking care of you and your relationship with God FIRST or stay in the cycle of being used and walked on by faithless friends and family. At the end of the day, it is always you and the God that never changes because of your bad decisions or empty pockets . . . He loves you beyond these simple folks and sorry circumstances.

Make this day the day you open up and trust God to grow you out of that cycle of bad choices, flaky friends and stifled praises.

He can and will meet you where you are.

Consider On This Day: An About Face Can Change Failed Directions

2 Chronicles 7:12–16

In some form or fashion, we have heard this scripture shouted out in prayer and in the church and never took time to see the history and background into why the Lord seeks for His Children to seek prosperous directions and agendas.

Leadership is one thing, but having an ability to step down from high places and take the backseat, one can learn a great deal of things by watching and listening. It is the example that gives those around us a clearance to speak and act at a certain level. All based on what they see in us. Solomon had taken a place in the congregation as worship leader and gave a prayer of supplication to the Lord in the sincere hope that God would bless the Children of Israel and continue to be with them no matter their choices. After all his heart-felt praying, Solomon found himself without a word to say when God appeared to Him the temple. God heard him and made mention of his prayer and desire.

Examples are those good things we see in others and then work to add them into our daily routines.

God hears all that we say to Him. The things that slow Him down from acting in our days are our inability to be faithful to Him and our families. God requires those who worship Him to be prepared to meet Him at His level and on His time. In chapter 6, all the people were at the correct place, the problem is they did not expect of God to be in the very place He created.

Verse 14 is the answer God gave to Solomon as a corrective measure in the in setting boundaries and getting the children of Israel to fellowship with Him all over again. No one person is above another based on person acts or merits: someone has gifted them that position and the image shown to others is what drives them away or pulls them in closer.

Leadership is a direct example. It offers insight to how the person is away from the group, the church or the job. God sets a standard and still requires that same standard in all of us. This is the mindset we should have in dealing with folks. Our standards have to be in line with God's in order for those who are not quite right and for those who can smell their own behinds and believe themselves to be great.

But all things still remain in the hands of the individual and his / her choices.

Consider On This Day: Results Matter

Reference Scripture: Colossians 2:1–9

Our approach toward friends and family do have a great weight on how successful they are in their attempts to either grow or reach the goals they have set for themselves & their families

Not all our family members and friends seek to move above the stationed in which they have been living. It is our desires to see them reach for the skies, so we pray and hope and hope and pray that they do not remain stuck on slow& satisfied

In the 2nd Chapter of Colossians, Paul is telling two churches that his prayers are set before the Lord concerning their successes in this world & that they become stronger in the Word. His example to us shows that visibility does not hinder a good prayer life and a short phone call or text to say -- I am praying for you and your family

Where we are in Christ has a great deal to do in how those who watch us move toward the church and then to Christ Jesus

Our results in keeping those we know and love encouraged should be seen in the responses and blessings God pours out on us for being ACTIVELY FAITHFUL toward His children. In order for us to keep reaching and moving, we must take serious moments in our quiet time so we can remain rooted and grounded in all areas of our lives. Our ability to allow others to see Christ in us depends upon how much of us is NOT in God's way

All the things that we would like to plan and do in the next 6 months and 6 years must be thought on, prayed over and planned out. If we do not begin now to set things in order, how will they work out when that they arrive?

Consider On This Day: Chasing Dreams and Purpose

During most of our days, we tend not to look back and study those things that we have gotten over and broken through because of the hurts and pangs that are associated with them. This is a problem that all may suffer from in one way or another. The best way to move and change the frame work and set patterns is refocusing.

Focus—is the ability to find a center line of interest in any singular activity and use that line to move into a clearer frame of thought and insight

Scripture:

I Chronicles 11:22–25 (read the scripture and think on what was accomplished)

Desires, Wants & Needs are the different levels one deals with on a day to day trek. The strange happenings in not acting correctly on either can cause the individual to lose ground in maturation and pursuit of goals.

The other side of pursuing dreams and goals is the two cents that is always offered and most times is contrary to what the individual has been praying on and for—and will consider that nonsense.

It is called being distracted.

Our need to become better pushes us to seek those things that will get us closer to our goals and dreams.

Our wants are settled in the animal-like instinct of conquering and subduing. This is the drive behind one overcoming obstacles and detours in life in order to clothe and feed family and spouse.

The portions of our days that are visions and dreams are based and wrapped in those desires.

Some come to fruition.

Some that remain visions and goals never pursued or accomplished for one reason or another.

In 1 Chronicles 11, the text shows us that there were certain individuals (Benaniah = ben a nye uh) who desired to be as good as the king and wanted to move into a greater fellowship with Him.

What is seen in each of them is their desires moved from dream to want to need. They fulfilled their needs through preparation and belief in their own talents and gifts.

Prayer, preparation and planning will get any individual from one level in life to another.

This is called being settled and focused.

The question remains—what is holding each person from obtaining and moving forward??